Poems for Squares

29 INSTAGRAM ACCOUNTS IN VERSE

Elyse Hart

LINT BALL
PRESS

LOS ANGELES, CA

Poems for Squares: 29 Instagram Accounts in Verse
by Elyse Hart

Cover and Interior Design: by Elyse Hart.

Published by Elyse Hart
www.elysehart.com

Copyright © 2023 Elyse Hart

All rights reserved. No portion of this book may be reproduced in any form without permission from the publisher, except as permitted by U.S. copyright law. For permissions contact: elysebhart@gmail.com.

ISBN: 978-0-578-27392-1 (print)

Printed in USA

1st Edition

For all who appear in this book.

Contents

Acknowledgments ix
About This Book xi
All the Mexicos 2
Dog People Want to be Cats 4
Visible Cities 6
Cottagecore Forever 8
Things Get Jesus-y in the Desert 10
In Effie's Eyes 12
A Cirque-us at Hogwarts 14
The Man Who Loved a Bus 16
Happy Birthday Rocket 18
Strut Tuscon in Gold Lamé 20
The DJ That Saved Our Youth 22
Do Touch the ART 24
Popsicle Is Driven to Drink 26
Pictures of Pictures of Paintings 28
Frame for Nothing 30
Make Sweet Sally Sing 32
A Hidden Kiss in the Land of X 34
You Are an Egg in My Family Tree 36
Bourbon Bluebonnet 38
Dance Like a Jacked-Up Bear? 40
This World Is Photogenic AF 42
A Train to Fame 44
Your Soup Is in the Mail 46
The Whole Role of Film 48
The Arbitrary Line 50
The Purple Beat 52
Build Your Blanky Fort in My Heart 54
The Long Hike 56
Give Me a Snail Funeral 58
About the Author 61
In Memoriam 63

Acknowledgments

My most heartfelt gratitude to everyone who participated and made this project possible. I'm touched that you asked me to write you a poem and allowed me to use your photographs for this book.

My thanks go to everyone who requested a poem:

Alexander Potts, Angela, Aryan, Ashley Jakubczyk, Caitlin Gemmell, Charlie Vargas, Caleb Knueven, Daria L., Diego Salinas Gardon, Eduardo Iniestra, Frederick C. Fajardo, Genevieve Kozlowski, Hillary & Popsicle the Cat, Justin Lenoir, Kara A. Clauser, Katelyn, Leslie Woodward, Lauren Bruniges, Lori Worley, Luke Smith, Movie Mike, Nyeema M LaMare, Rena Elizabeth, Rich Ferguson, Santiago Pichardo, Shivika, Tiffany Quevedo, and Vanessa Murillo.

Special thanks to Mikey Smith for design consultation.

Thanks also to:

Alexis Rhone Fancher for use of her photograph of Rich Ferguson on page 33.

Brisaela Rose and Emma Dean (@brizzyroseandemma) for use of their photograph in the upper right quadrant of page 27.

About This Book

A few years ago, I posted on Instagram that I would write a poem about anyone who asked me to. The poem would be inspired by their Instagram photos. After writing a few for people I knew, I started to receive requests from their followers—and a chain effect began.

I started an Instagram account (@elysehartpoetry) dedicated to these and other poems. When I ended the project, I had written 29 poems in all. Some for people I knew, others for people I came to know through their photos.

These poems are my imaginings of what these Instagram photos are about and the significance of these particular moments to the individual.

My aim in writing these poems was to delight the people who received them. I did not originally set out to create a book, but I eventually figured these poems belong in some sort of compilation.

For simplicity, I have featured only four photos per poem. Some poems were based on more than four photos. If you find each verse doesn't correspond with a photo, let the poem guide your imagination!

I hope you enjoy these poems as I have enjoyed writing them. I continue to post poetry content on my Instagram account, so follow me @elysehartpoetry.

See you on Instagram!

Poems for Squares

All the Mexicos

for Kara A. Clauser

Like a page torn out of the sky
mountains climb above our
bobbing heads engulfed in gulf.

Trek through
Mexicos old and new
surprises frosting-painted
on faces,

constrictors like unfeathered boas
round the shoulders
in the green haze of
underground passageways—

exchanges go on for days
or minutes, or,
I don't know man,
I lost count.

In April, there aren't showers
but growls—

these dogs are chillin',
they're like my children
but their daddies
are all passed out
on my living room floor.

@karaclaws

Dog People Want to Be Cats

for Diego Salinas Gardon

I sent whispers down
dark country roads,
border collies trailed
in tracks of greater beasts.

I knew not for what I searched,
just that I felt incomplete.

Behind our masks,
we are not fierce
not cunning, not lovely—
we are wholly human:

imperfect creatures
grasping into night,
the shrieks of inner children
piercing the navy sky.

But with a mask,
we are who we like—
and can we agree?
Most people want to be cats.

Dog people want to be cats,
for what does being a dog get you
in this dog-smell-dog-butt world?

But to be a cat!
To shred your enemies to ribbons
and only on occasion endure
being dressed in silly outfits—

Oh, forgive me my trespass,
Filemona!

@entrompadoroteo

Visible Cities

for Nyeema M LaMare

You walk three days
through forest and mist,
come upon a vertical city
that shines like gold on a hill.

The doorknobs of every home
carry a patina.
The dogs whisper to one another:
"autumn, it's autumn, autumn!
AUTUMN!"

Their snouts inhale
sweet crushed leaves

while the cats are less enthused—
they whisper disapproval of
superfluous matters;
they are outside the circle of
changing seasons.

Luna, a circle of fluffy snow
reminds me of when
the clouds rolled in—
white, not gray, that day

at the beach and driftwood
crawled up on the sand.
It whispered—"I'm alive!"
though it was not.

Perhaps it lived
in those far-off huts

or maybe they were just rocks,
"just" rocks.

@dakini_wahine

Cottagecore Forever

for Caitlin Gemmell

Handful of blue florets
five petals
dusting my life, my
love line, my
tea leaves read
enchanted simplicity, my
basket heaves
with scraps we've
scraped with our
two hands to eat
of the earth, my
feet touch the land
where stumps erupt
and stones are sprinkled
and placed
just so as I hold
a wood thrush
in my hands.

@caitlin.gemmell

Things Get Jesus-y in the Desert

for Caleb Knueven

Empty is this place
the guts disgraced,
the armchair concerned
with eschatology.

God is love God is
my church in tow
on a broken down truck
tattooed in repentance and sin.

The desert is barren and grim,
we stare to the sky,
let light make shapes
on our retinas
and if one of them
looks like Jesus on toast,
then, hallelujah!

They left the trailer
when life became all
Bud Light and chili beans—

a lens flare will bring beauty
to this scene.

When X marks the spot,
follow it to the heart,
'cause for chrissake God is love!

No really—GOD IS LOVE!!

We paint the desert our palette
of blood of Christ and holy ghost.

Drive out here and revere
the flag, the cross, the Bible—
across the street
the lone tree and forgotten tires.

@calebknueven

In Effie's Eyes

for Lauren Bruniges

Lights, action.

Lost my way but found again
in a world gone mad,
or was it I who did?
Either way,
I look cute doing it.

Heterochromic kitty,
absorber of rainbows—
don't get near
unless you're mommy
'cause she'll swipe your ass.

Pinching Taj by the nip,
tartan, used to look like a kid
on a Christmas morn'
but now hot as shit.

Boss girl plays the players
all in bangs
and a fuzzy sweater.

@lbruniges

A Cirque-us at Hogwarts

for Tiffany Quevedo

Spotlight you Cursed Child—
hold me close
in the Niagra terminal,
in Buffalo.

Dressed for war
if war is a painted flight
against Time.

Columnal commencement
at Columbia calls
of springtime climes

while Paula's pancakes
pass as prime.

Luzia, my darling!
a dream of acrobats and mimes—
fantástico!

But not so much as
this shiny new ride,
a new year deserves a new chariot
to ride into the dawn

while first-time pies
pluck of Martha Stewart vibes.

The Man Who Loved a Bus

for Movie Mike

I like old Hollywood charm—
martinis served dry,
waitstaff draped in satin lapels.

I like memories I can feel
in my palm, imbued
with the weight of history—
talismans of the past.

Fifteen years is a long time
without you, my dear
but as you roll into the golden light
of afternoon,
ever-creamy and glowing,
your neck and feet
peacock-jeweled and eager—

I delight in knowing the wait,
that epic wait
to ride you is over.

You shall call me a happy man.
and I shall call you
my '61 VW panel.

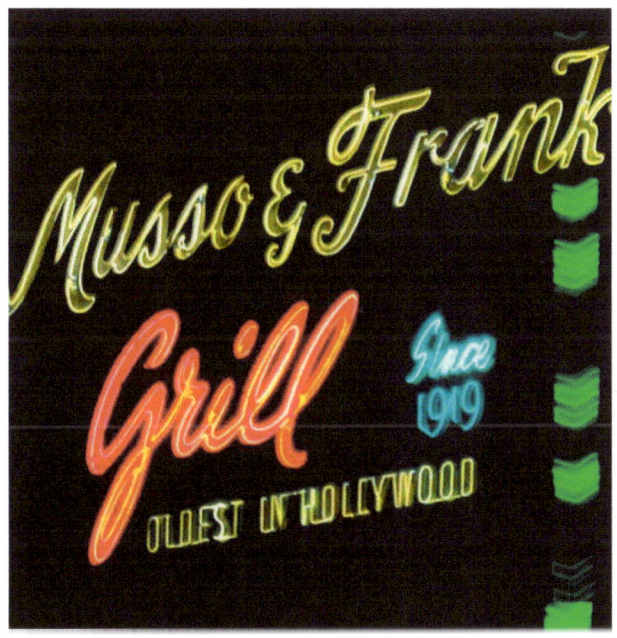

@scopicdrive

Happy Birthday Rocket

for Shivika

She celebrates
on a bed of roses
the twentieth anniversary
of her birth

with a rocket shooting
its sparkle
skyward.

And cake,
there's got to be cake.

This Indian princess
plays Native American princess—
a feather dangles
down her cheek,

down her hair,
its blackness stretches
on for miles.

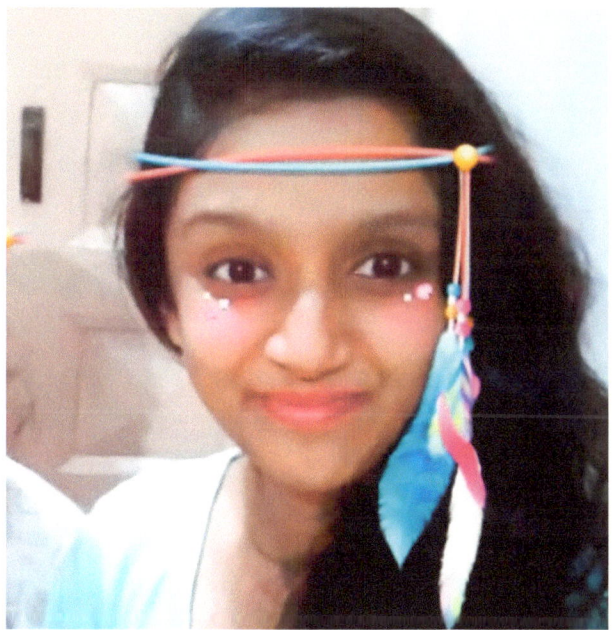

@shivi2519

Strut Tuscon in Gold Lamé

for Santiago Pichardo

Bolts are the illusion of safety,
but you're not safe
unless you're huddled
in April's warm embrace.

E-cigs are just a ploy
for the electric company
to charge you
to charge more—
dat ass, tho!
Unscheduled as it is bare.

Julio who drives the van—
Julio who?
The ice cream man!

When we die,
our bodies become the grass,
the antelope eat the grass
and then our skeletons ride bikes
all around Tucson.

Pretty in pink,
a posey-crowned princess
points at bees' wings.

I look good in gold lamé on a crate,
the crate on holy ground,
waiting for I don't know what
but my cigarette is charged.

Yeah, I eat granola
but it's not vegan,
this granola's the real shit.

I smoke blunts as big as forearms
with a side of Mickey's and wieners,
no buns—

but at the end of the day
I do the good work
saving little tortoises
from fate.

@santopinche

The DJ Who Saved Our Youth

for Eduardo Iniestra

Expectant for the Angels
young and old,
our favorite pastime:
kick, snare, tom
(and ramen if you dare).

S.O.Y. kids tearin' it up—
behind it all:

the gray-suited master,
the teacher
the big believer
in the next generation
of beat-tappers,
synth-wackers,
LP-scratchers.

The air begs music
from our heads
born of our souls—
drawing it out by the love
we pass down to our own.

May DREAMERS keep dreaming
and canaries sing
their regal song.

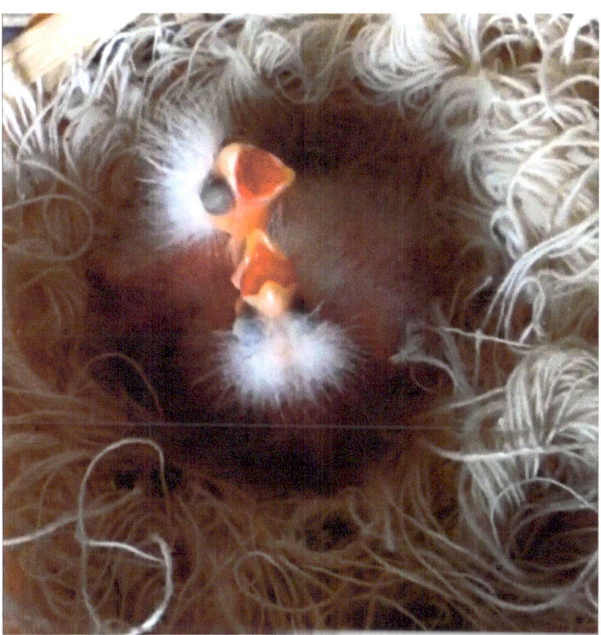

@therealdjkaboom

Do Touch the ART

for Vanessa Murillo

I got bangs for days,
loving myself in all new ways.
I've grown wings
and sometimes fly
over the beach,
my toes dragging through sand,
penning messages
of love and peace
as my skirt flutters,
floral in the salt breeze.

I touch the ART,
at least I touch the T in ART—
it wouldn't fly in a museum
but here I am down
by the Riverside,
touching that T.

An arrow is like a T
with slanted eaves,
mine points to my sisters,

and theirs to me—
these points skewer our
forever entwined hearts.

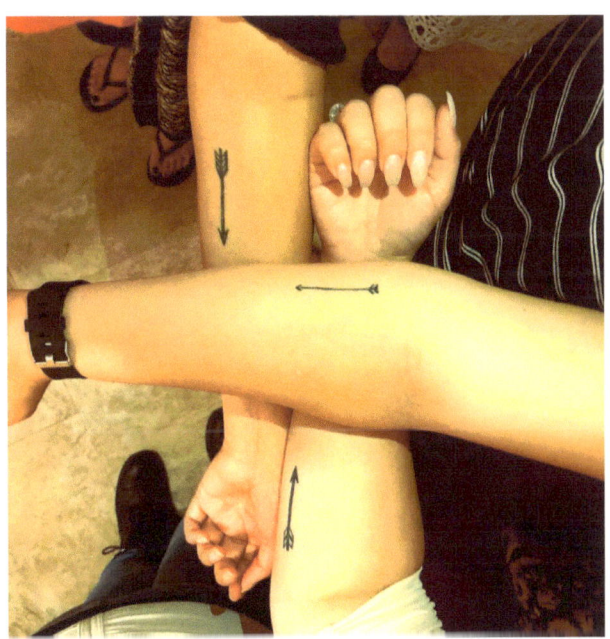

@marinessaposa

Popsicle Is Driven to Drink

for Hillary and Popsicle the Cat

Got a face like an 80-year-old,
water-loving,
my Maine man.

Pop loves that water,
from the jar,
from the sink—

got a haircut
like a half-shorn sheep.

beggar of treats,
smart as can be,
lover of all peeps.

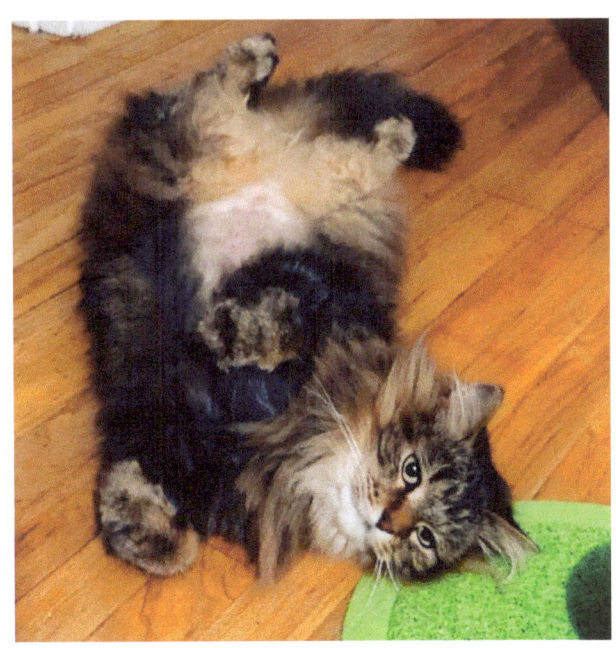
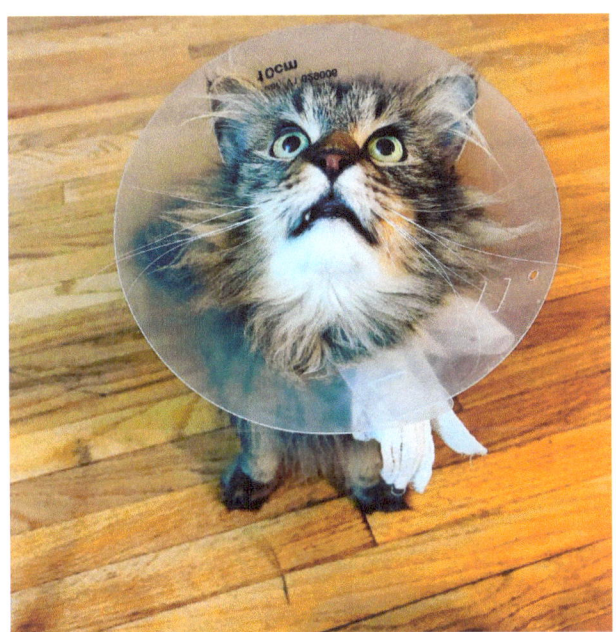

@popsicle.cat

Pictures of Pictures of Paintings

for Frederick C. Fajardo

Lavish in furs, amber brocade,
seashell pearls in titian curls.
Glass amulet kisses her
throat hollow,

coral seed rounds her collar.
Amid taffeta bows
the throws of sorrow take her.
Not the finest mink

nor tangled jacquard
enlivens her.
She is melancholy's mistress,
the woman trapped indoors.

Yet the goose girl who herds,
romps out-of-doors and
feels the sun blanket her skin
knows no pins in her heart.

Her hair mousy,
her skirts rough,
she sits among wildflowers
and talks to ducks.

She roams the plains
among cows that low—
she is happy,
her freedom in tow.

Frame for Nothing

for Rich Ferguson

If you put a frame around nothing, it becomes something. If you remove a fork's tines, it knows the phantom pain of an amputee or one whose heart was excised in a careless game of Operation.

If you encircle a candle in a festive paper orb, the fire desires to turn that bright piece of life to ash. The ashes of that celebration desire to make love with the wind—a new celebration of love, of beauty—munay, all one thing in Quechua.

A poor translation is a weak substitute for sitting in the full understanding of a word, its nuances, its labyrinthine meanderings through your neural network, the associations and aspirations of a single word. A concept.

If you stare into a rose, your traits fall between the petals, your memories absorbed by the stem, pumped through its leaves, your pain taken by the thorns. If someone plucks your rose and wears it in their hat, they step inside you, into a once-secret place. they inhabit or invade. You are altered.

If the hat is blown away by the wind and carried down the mountain, it will be caught by a stream and happily chewed by a llama. That wilted rose is your new beginning. The traits, the memories, the pain may build anew. Start over.

@fergiebeat

Make Sweet Sally Sing

for Alexander Potts

Can't contain my swagger,
dressed all in black
my ax sings,

it warbles and rings
by the blue light
as I lay down notes
that speak my song

and if I've gone
you'll know
it's 'cause I'm a
Deadman.

Before the stars and stripes
my rib cage displayed
and unbroken,

I pick my way through
Sally's wire hair,
I lick up and down
her wooden neck,

I don't fret
but my fingers tickle and rock
her wooden body.

@adp333

A Hidden Kiss in the Land of X

for Aryan

A hand reaches out
from tangled roots,
from the unknown,
from the land of X.

It's a pleading hand,
a begging hand,
a hand without country
without identity—

an identity half peeks out
beneath a stroke of hair
obscuring a kiss
that wants to be seen.

Your Are an Egg in My Family Tree

for Leslie Woodward

Tumble down my family tree,
do flips around my heart, big sis.

A bunny's a baby brandishing
a basket of bountiful eggs—
blue, pink, and silver.

All the waters are holy,
they wash their blessing over me.
Whether I am in sea
or stream-lit waters
where otters play,
there's no need to fear, my dear.

Obedience mastered—
pup in tasseled cap
looking quite dapper.

We're proud of our own,
our family has grown,
and so has the warmth
in our souls.

@woodwardles

Bourbon Bluebonnet

for Angela

Found my heart
in a cup of ceramic,
got a thing for bourbon,
not manic—

Dallas gal in Texan Bluebonnet,
unexpected bursting
from plain ol' grass—
(big things happen in small places).

Surely those Furs are cruelty-free
but they're still Psychedelic,
got a daughter like
the princess of Argos
about to graduate.

Faces are better in quadrants,
eye up there, lips down where,
cross-hatch, probably Haring,
broad and undespairing

but spring comes alive
in the orange tendrils
of a solitary bell bloom.

@angelaanable

Dance Like a Jacked-Up Bear

for Charlie Vargas

A bloodied lip
born of a mosh pit—
if you ask why I dance
like a jacked-up bear I'll say:
the devil made me do it.

You like your fiction with
or without pulp?
I like mine on a tee.

The house whose windows are eyes
sees us on the boardwalk,
rollerblading. On the sand side,
a station guards our pride—
but unmanned, who will save us?

If mirrors are portals,
I'm bringing skinny ties
to the 17th century.

Who holds the key
to this boundless reverie—
a vision of you before my bay?

Ground beef can buy you a slice,
but only from people
who are plenty stoned
and plenty nice.

@cheerupcharlie_

This World Is Photogenic AF

for Genevieve Kozlowski

I live this moment
in the garden of life,
a garden like an easterly island
where I walk the path of eternity
and look good doing it—

photogenic as fuck,
calla lily so graceful
swirls its petals for me,

river cuts through trees
sunflower envelops bee.
Knee deep in winter snow,

evergreen needles tell tales
of corgi tails and
Bandit bares a grin.

The horizon burns a sunset
into the surf
fleeting in magnificence,

time sifting through
our clutching hands
like so many granules of sand

and the sun keeps setting—
over Melrose Ave,
over my head,
behind the mountains

while I stand to see it all
from a field of flowers.

@genevievekozlowski

A Train to Fame

for Ashley Jakubczyk

Confetti carousel
skewers my heart;
oysters, crabs, and clams
hit The Spot.

Succulents sit just so
while shelves at Powell's
await my masterpiece.

I stand in squares,
in cubes, in hexagons.
On leaves, red and green.

I stand on earth looking
to the river, looking to
totems marking
the sky against time.

I ride on trains and rafts
and bridges. I'm traveling
to where the rushes grow
to where the coast guard rows

to a table where
I find Strength,

to where the forest lets peek
its seedlings reaching
their green toward the blue.

Your Soup Is in the Mail

for Luke Smith

Darth, ginger snaps, and time
to unwind my mind,
to wind my watch,
to unmind my words
which are by _____.

My cause célèbre
are cranes in the mist,
flight over a cornfield.

If your head is made of blocks
blockhead is not an insult.
Blocks are not like any moon,
a backlit drachma,
disc-shaped or a bowl of soup

to be eaten with a spoon
and sent off through the post,
slipped through a slot
of a red mailbox—

that will surprise the host.

@ls_wordy

The Whole Role of Film

for Caleb Knueven

Green cab red hitch
ain't going nowhere
on those flat tires.

Lime green tile screams
at tiny pink hairdryer,
not packing many RPMs
for that half-dried, humid look.

Monkeys drink bottled water—
tap water doesn't cut it
for a monkey these days.

And photos aren't just
for Instagram,
they're printed and hung
in the Annenberg Space—

of once a place
where children happily peed
in chlorinated sun-soaked waters,

reborn as somewhere
spray-art dwells in sandy vastness.

@calebknueven

The Arbitrary Line

for Daria L.

Water, mud, water, mud:
two ends of the spectrum of purity.

The towers glitter
against a starless sky,
the gap is bridged by the teaching
of this universal language.

On the sky deck,
I see to infinity, skylifted
toward the green horizon—

a perfect waterfall, a perfect cloud,
too much for one day.

I live the jungle life of flamingoes,
lagoons, and lilypads,

my view is littered
with white horses,
waterfalls and parakeets—

I'm like a Snow White
with the birds,
the deer—

they're all spirit animals
and I am their guardian.

But I got more deer friends
than I can handle,
so I'll just hang with
this brass snail instead.

Look out at the rainbowed waters
over river Cau:
I stay where nature converges
with the buzz of the city—

are these habitats truly different
or is this an arbitrary line we draw?

@daria_uneven

The Purple Beat

for Justin Lenoir

Window casts a shadow
like an echo across
a papered wall—
it illuminates my attitude.

My sticks are poised,
my foot on the kick,
in rhythm there's glue
holding you to the groove
resounding.

LA sun reflects in my eyes,
I'm basking in the life,
the city crops up around me—
I'm of it, in it,
and it's in me.

I don't question Iris—
she's purple and so's the venue.
Candelabras are glowing,
I tap the hi-hat:

a tintinnabulation
in a field of books—
a breadcrumb, a siren
that leads me where I'm going.

@justinlenoir

Build Your Blanky Fort in My Heart

for Rena Elizabeth

Table high, dance
in purple shadows—
choreograph my heart
within a blanky fortress,
a secret world of tiny feet
and Magna Doodle.

Giraffes ride my handlebars,
in this world there's much
to go "rawr!" at.

If your eyes are turning to bone
I shall kiss and heal thee.

And I wanted to tell you:
happy new year.
happy new year—
happy new year,
happy new year!
HAPPY NEW YEAR

@renaelizabeth

The Long Hike

for Katelyn

Cactus full of snow
an unwelcome guest
to butterfly babes.

Love is a long straw
in a chalice of juice
and alcohol—

a straw connects us,
encircles us all
in regretless union.

If harsh words come to the
precipice of your lips,
they're hushed

by a floral-donned beauty's first
understanding of the aroma
of bride's bouquets

of which she has many miles
to hike before she'll catch.

@kclauser

Give Me a Snail Funeral

for Lori Worley

Maraschino jubilee
red light drink special

old-fashioneds are in fashion,
so cheers!

Many have padded down
these dunes between moss
like bushy animals.

There's no bay beautiful enough
to solve all life's problems

even if the answers are in the mist,
they're unreachable by rowboat.

A little girl is growing up,
I can see her there—

watching herself
in the lighted mirror
unaware she'll one day be grown.

When I die, I want to get slimed
by all the people I have known

like snails do
mourning their own.

When I die, I'll want for nothing.

@author_loriworley

About the Author

Elyse Hart is a writer from Los Angeles where she lives with her cats, Asher and Fiona Apple. She is the author of the chapbook White Noise Crucible (Bottlecap Press). Her poems have been featured in publications including Slipstream, The Nervous Breakdown, Ghost City Review, Maudlin House, and others. You can find more of her work on Instagram @elysehartpoetry or at www.elysehart.com.

In Memoriam

My cat Genevieve appears on the cover and on the previous page. She passed peacefully at home on 11.11.2022 while this book was being created. She gave me 15-1/2 years of love and loyal companionship. May she rest in peace.

www.ingramcontent.com/pod-product-compliance
Lightning Source LLC
Chambersburg PA
CBHW041202290426
44109CB00003B/107